HIPPOS

by Jaclyn Jaycox

PEBBLE
a capstone imprint

Published by Pebble, an imprint of Capstone
1710 Roe Crest Drive, North Mankato, Minnesota 56003
capstonepub.com

Copyright © 2022 by Capstone. All rights reserved. No part of this publication may be reproduced in whole or in part, or stored in a retrieval system, or transmitted in any form or by any means, electronic, mechanical, photocopying, recording, or otherwise, without written permission of the publisher.

Library of Congress Cataloging-in-Publication Data
Names: Jaycox, Jaclyn, 1983– author.
Title: Hippos / by Jaclyn Jaycox.
Description: North Mankato, Minnesota : Pebble, [2022] | Series: Animals | Includes bibliographical references and index. | Audience: Ages 5–8 | Audience: Grades K–1 | Summary: "Hippos are one of the largest land mammals in the world! These big vegetarians prefer to spend their time in the water. Readers will enjoy learning more about hippos with exciting facts and vibrant photos."— Provided by publisher.
Identifiers: LCCN 2021028236 (print) | LCCN 2021028237 (ebook) | ISBN 9781663971883 (hardcover) | ISBN 9781666325713 (paperback) | ISBN 9781666325720 (pdf) | ISBN 9781666325744 (kindle edition)
Subjects: LCSH: Hippopotamus—Juvenile literature.
Classification: LCC QL737.U57 J39 2022 (print) | LCC QL737.U57 (ebook) | DDC 599.63/5—dc23
LC record available at https://lccn.loc.gov/2021028236
LC ebook record available at https://lccn.loc.gov/2021028237e.

Image Credits
Alamy: frans lemmens, 28; Shutterstock: Andrew Nicholas White, 11, Benjamin B, 5, BlueOrange Studio, 10, Brian Divelbiss, 9, Bruce Ellis, 23, Carl Dawson, 17, DM Meadows, 26, Gaston Piccinetti, Cover, Karel Stipek, 27, Kelly Ermis, 19, MyImages - Micha, 15, PACO COMO, 14, Revival Design, 21, SebastiaanPeeters, 13, sirtravelalot, 12, slowmotiongli, 7, Snapper Nick, 22, Stu Porter, 8, 18, 25, Volodymyr Burdiak, 1, 24

Editorial Credits
Editors: Gena Chester and Abby Huff; Designer: Dina Her;
Media Researcher: Jo Miller; Production Specialist: Tori Abraham

All internet sites appearing in back matter were available and accurate when this book was sent to press.

Printed in the United States 5702

Table of Contents

Words in **bold** are in the glossary.

Amazing Hippos

There is an animal that spends a lot of time in the water. Can you guess what it is? It's a hippopotamus! It's called a hippo for short.

Hippos are one of the largest land animals. They are **mammals**. They breathe air. They have hair. They give birth to live young.

Where in the World

There are two kinds of hippos. One is the common hippo. The other is the pygmy hippo. Both are found in Africa. Some hippos live in forests. Others live in grasslands. All live near water.

Hippos Range Map

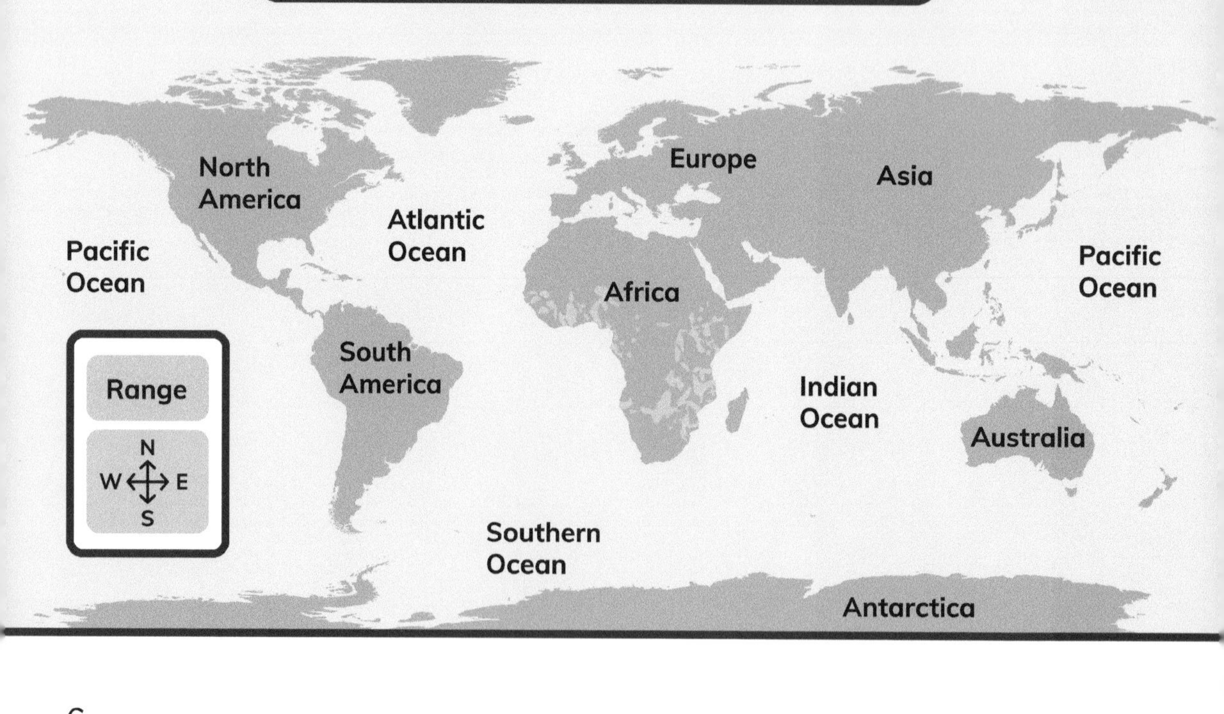

Pygmy hippos are rarer and smaller than common hippos.

Hippo **habitats** are very hot. But hippos don't sweat. Instead, they use water to cool off. Their skin also makes a red slime. The slime looks like blood! It keeps the skin wet. It keeps hippos from getting sunburned.

Common hippos are large and have long faces.

Hippos are **semi-aquatic**. They live on land. But they spend up to 16 hours a day in the water. They even sleep in the water. You can find hippos in swamps, lakes, and rivers. Birds and turtles often sit on their backs.

After the sun sets, hippos come on land to eat. They are most active at night.

Huge Hippos

Hippos are huge! Common hippos are bigger than pygmy hippos. They can be 6 to 16.5 feet (1.8 to 5 meters) long. They grow up to 5 feet (1.5 m) tall. They can weigh more than 3.5 tons. That is almost twice as heavy as a car!

Hippos are big. But they are not slow! They can run up to 30 miles (48 kilometers) per hour.

Hippos are made for the water. They have short, strong legs. They have **webbed** toes. This makes it easy to move through water.

A hippo's eyes, ears, and nostrils are on the top of its head. The hippo can go mostly underwater. But it can still see, hear, and breathe!

Hippos sink under the water when they sleep. Their ears and nostrils close. They can hold their breath for five minutes. Then hippos float to the surface without waking to breathe.

Hippos have grayish-brown skin. But their stomachs and parts of their faces are pink. They have some hair. It grows on their heads and tails.

Hippos have big mouths that open wide. Their teeth can grow longer than a bowling pin. They use their teeth to fight off enemies.

Hippos have flat tails. Males use their tails to throw their poop! The poop marks their **territory**. It tells other male hippos to stay away.

On the Menu

When it's dark, it's time to eat! Hippos usually stay near the water. But they will go farther if food is hard to find.

Hippos eat grass and leaves. They eat other small plants and fruit too. Hippos don't use their teeth. They grab grass with their strong lips.

Each night, hippos eat around 80 pounds (36 kilograms) of food. That might seem like a lot. But it's not much for such a big animal!

Hippos are not very active. So they don't need a lot of food. Sometimes food is hard to find. Hippos can keep two days' worth of grass in their stomachs. They can go up to three weeks without eating.

Life of a Hippo

Hippos live in groups called **herds**. Usually, about 10 to 30 hippos are in one herd. They grunt and snort to each other. They are very loud. Their sounds can get about as loud as a rock concert!

Hippos usually **mate** during the dry season. This is from February to August. It does not rain much in this time. Females carry their young for eight months.

Females leave the herd to give birth. They have one baby at a time. Baby hippos are called calves. They are often born in the water. Calves can weigh up to 100 pounds (45 kg).

The baby can drink milk from its mother underwater. It can hold its breath for about 40 seconds. It sleeps on its mother's back when it needs to rest.

After a week or so, the calf is stronger. The mother and baby join the herd. The group helps keep the baby safe from **predators**.

Calves drink their mother's milk for almost a year. Hippos stay with their mothers until they are fully grown. This can take about eight years. They live about 40 years in the wild.

Dangers to Hippos

Lions, hyenas, and crocodiles hunt younger hippos. Calves are also in danger when adult hippos fight. They can be bitten or hit by mistake.

Adult hippos don't have many predators. Their biggest danger is humans. Hippos are losing their homes. More land that they live on is being used for farming.

Some people hunt hippos for their meat and teeth. It is against the law to sell hippo teeth. But people do it anyway.

Pygmy hippos are in danger of dying out. Fewer than 3,000 are left. The number of common hippos is also going down.

People are trying to help hippos. Some are making stronger hunting laws. Other people are working to protect land where hippos live.

Fast Facts

Name: hippopotamus, or hippo for short

Habitat: grasslands and forests, near rivers, swamps, and lakes

Where in the World: Africa

Food: grass, leaves, plants, fruit

Predators: lions, hyenas, crocodiles, humans

Life Span: about 40 years

Glossary

habitat (HAB-uh-tat)—where a plant or animal lives

herd (HURD)—a large group of animals that lives or moves together

mammal (MAM-uhl)—a warm-blooded animal that breathes air; mammals usually have hair or fur; female mammals feed milk to their young

mate (MEYT)—to join with another to produce young

predator (PRED-uh-tur)—an animal that hunts other animals for food

semi-aquatic (seh-mee-uh-KWAH-tik)—growing or living in water most, but not all, of the time

territory (TER-uh-tor-ee)—the land on which an animal finds food and where it raises its young

webbed (WEBD)—having folded skin or tissue between the toes or fingers

Read More

Hansen, Grace. *Hippopotamus*. Minneapolis: Abdo Kids, 2018.

Levy, Janey. *Hippos vs. Polar Bear*. New York: Gareth Stevens Publishing, 2018.

Nelson, Penelope. *Hippopotamuses*. Minneapolis: Jump! Inc., 2019.

Internet Sites

DK FindOut!: Hippopotamuses
dkfindout.com/us/animals-and-nature/hippopotamuses/

National Geographic Kids: 10 Hippo Facts!
natgeokids.com/ie/discover/animals/general-animals/ten-hippo-facts/

San Diego Zoo Kids: River Hippo
kids.sandiegozoo.org/animals/river-hippo

Index

About the Author

Jaclyn Jaycox is a children's book author and editor. She lives in southern Minnesota with her husband, two kids, and a spunky goldendoodle.

PANGOLINS

by Jaclyn Jaycox

PEBBLE
a capstone imprint

Published by Pebble, an imprint of Capstone
1710 Roe Crest Drive, North Mankato, Minnesota 56003
capstonepub.com

Copyright © 2022 by Capstone. All rights reserved. No part of this publication may be reproduced in whole or in part, or stored in a retrieval system, or transmitted in any form or by any means, electronic, mechanical, photocopying, recording, or otherwise, without written permission of the publisher.

Library of Congress Cataloging-in-Publication Data
Names: Jaycox, Jaclyn, 1983– author.
Title: Pangolins / by Jaclyn Jaycox.
Description: North Mankato, Minnesota : Pebble, [2022] | Series: Animals | Includes bibliographical references and index. | Audience: Ages 5–8 | Audience: Grades K–1 | Summary: "Pangolins' bodies are a rare sight. They have scales and claws! Bright photos bring these unusual mammals to life. Readers will follow along with easy-to-read text and will enjoy learning all they can about pangolins."— Provided by publisher.
Identifiers: LCCN 2021029749 (print) | LCCN 2021029750 (ebook) | ISBN 9781663971753 (hardcover) | ISBN 9781666325638 (paperback) | ISBN 9781666325645 (pdf) | ISBN 9781666325669 (kindle edition)
Subjects: LCSH: Pangolins—Juvenile literature.
Classification: LCC QL737.P5 J39 2022 (print) | LCC QL737.P5 (ebook) | DDC 599.3/1—dc23
LC record available at https://lccn.loc.gov/2021029749
LC ebook record available at https://lccn.loc.gov/2021029750

Image Credits
Alamy: George Philip, 7, Jiri Prochazka, 1, 9, 23, Mint Images Limited, 14, Nature Picture Library, 12, roger allen, 28; Newscom: Photoshot/NHPA/Anthony Bannister, 18, Photoshot/NHPA/Daryl Balfour, 24, ZUMA Press/Afrianto Silalahl, 27; Shutterstock: Holly Auchincloss, 26, Joel Alves, 11, Nick Greaves, 10, paula french, 13, Positive Snapshot, 21, Rich Lindie, 8, 17, Vickey Chauhan, 5, Cover

Editorial Credits
Editors: Gena Chester and Abby Huff; Designer: Dina Her;
Media Researcher: Jo Miller; Production Specialist: Tori Abraham

All internet sites appearing in back matter were available and accurate when this book was sent to press.

Printed and bound in the USA. PO4608

Table of Contents

Words in **bold** are in the glossary.

Amazing Pangolins

A strange creature walks by. It has scales all over its body. It has long front claws. Is it a dinosaur? No, it's a pangolin!

Don't let the scales fool you. These animals are **mammals**. They breathe air. They give birth to live young. There are eight kinds of pangolins.

Where in the World

Four kinds are found in Africa. They are the white-bellied, black-bellied, giant, and ground pangolins. The other four live in Asia. They are the Chinese, Sunda, Indian, and Philippine pangolins.

Pangolin Range Map

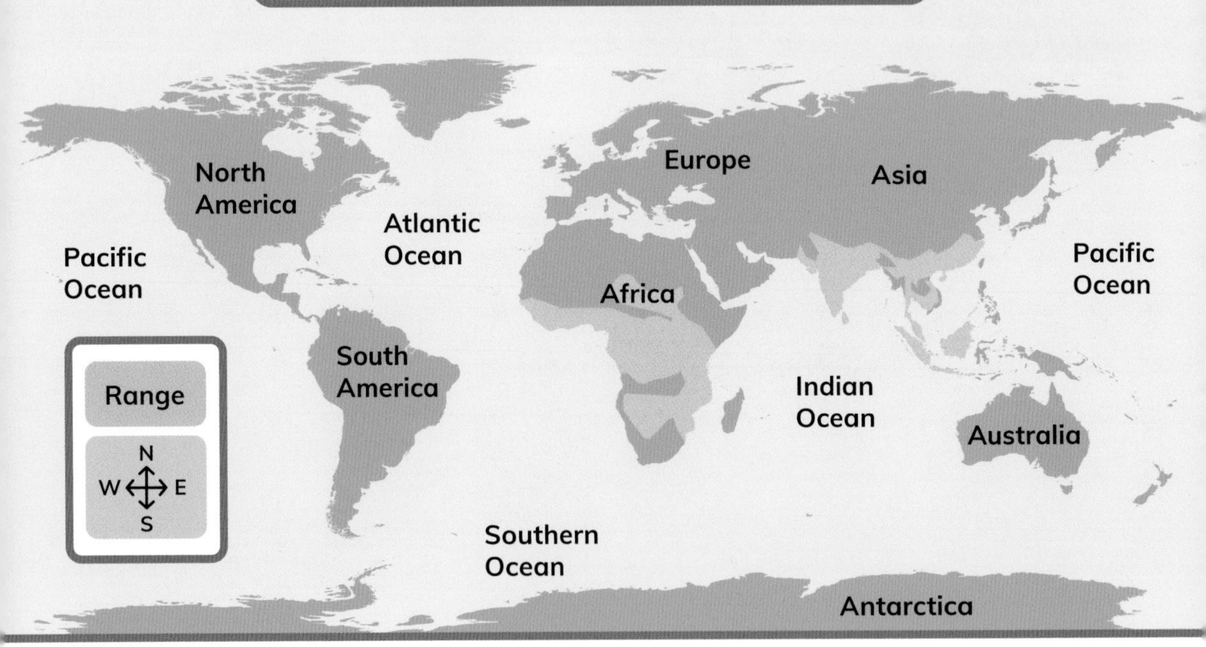

ground pangolin

Pangolins make homes in many **habitats**. They live in **tropical** forests and grasslands. They live in swamps and deserts too.

Pangolins are **nocturnal**. They rest during the day. They are active at night. Many live on the ground. They sleep in large **burrows**. They may dig their own. Sometimes they use ones left by other animals.

Some pangolins are good climbers.
They live up in trees. They sleep there too.

Pangolin Bodies

Pangolins are special. No other mammal has scales from head to tail! The scales can be brown or olive green. They blend in with the ground and plants.

Pangolins roll up into a ball when in danger. Their scales are tough. They act like armor. They keep the animal safe from **predators**. Pangolins will also swing their tail. The sharp scales can hurt attackers.

These critters are many sizes. The smallest is the black-bellied pangolin. It grows about 2.5 feet (0.8 meters) long. That's about the size of a big house cat. The largest is the giant pangolin. It can grow up to 6 feet (1.8 m) long.

Pangolins have long front claws. These are good for digging. They also help climb trees. But the claws can make it hard to walk. So pangolins will sometimes walk on their back legs. Their tails help them balance.

Pangolins have long and pointy faces. They have small eyes. Their tongues are very long. Most animals have tongues that start in the mouth. But a pangolin's tongue starts under the rib cage. It can be longer than the whole body!

On the Menu

The sun has set. A pangolin crawls out of its burrow. It's time for dinner!

Pangolins eat ants and termites. And they eat a lot! These animals eat up to 70 million **insects** each year.

Pangolins can't see well. They use their strong sense of smell to find **prey**. They sniff out ant and termite nests. They use their big claws to dig inside.

A pangolin digs for insects.

These animals don't have teeth. Their long tongues reach into insect nests. Insects stick to the tongue. The pangolin pulls up the food. It has special muscles in its mouth. This keeps prey from crawling out. It swallows the food whole.

Insects climb all over the pangolin while it eats. To stay safe, pangolins can close their nose and ears. This keeps insects out.

Life of a Pangolin

Pangolins live alone. They only come together to **mate**. Females usually have one baby at a time. But some kinds may have two or three. Males don't help care for young.

Females make a nest in their burrow. They give birth there. Babies are very small. They are about 6 inches (15 centimeters) long. They are white. Their scales are soft. Over a few days, the scales harden. They turn brown.

a young Indian pangolin

The mother stays in the burrow with her baby. She keeps it warm. If danger is near, she curls up around the baby. This keeps the baby safe.

The baby drinks milk from its mother. After about a month, the baby is ready to leave the burrow. It starts to eat prey. But it still drinks milk for up to four months. The mother hunts for food. The baby rides on her tail.

Mothers care for young until they are adults. Then they go their own ways. Pangolins are adults when they are ready to mate. This takes about two years.

Scientists are not sure how long these animals live in the wild. Some pangolins cared for by humans have lived up to 20 years.

Dangers to Pangolins

Lions, leopards, and hyenas hunt pangolins. But humans are their biggest threat.

Scales that were being sold illegally

It's against the law to hunt pangolins. But people do it anyway. They are one of the most **illegally** caught animals in the world. People use their scales in medicines. They eat their meat.

The number of pangolins is going down. They are in danger of dying out. But people are working to help them.

Stronger laws are being passed against hunting. China no longer allows the scales to be used in medicines. Many groups are teaching others how important these amazing animals are.

Fast Facts

Name: pangolin

Habitat: tropical forests, grasslands, deserts, swamps

Where in the World: Asia, Africa

Food: ants, termites

Predators: lions, leopards, hyenas, humans

Life Span: unknown; up to 20 years in captivity

Glossary

burrow (BUHR-oh)—a hole or tunnel in the ground made or used by an animal

habitat (HAB-uh-tat)—where a plant or animal lives

illegally (ih-LEE-guh-lee)—done against the law

insect (IN-sekt)—a small animal with a hard outer shell, six legs, three body sections, and two antennae

mammal (MAM-uhl)—a warm–blooded animal that breathes air; mammals usually have hair or fur; females feed milk to their young

mate (MEYT)—to join with another to produce young

nocturnal (nok-TUR-nuhl)—active at night and resting during the day

predator (PRED-uh-tur)—an animal that hunts other animals for food

prey (PRAY)—an animal hunted by another animal for food

tropical (TROP-ih-kuhl)—having to do with the hot and wet areas near the equator

Read More

Hansen, Grace. *Pangolin*. Edina, MN: Abdo Kids, 2021.

Kline, Carol. *All About Asian Pangolins*. Hallandale, FL: Mitchell Lane Publishers, 2019.

Marsh, Laura. *Animal Armor*. Washington, D.C.: National Geographic, 2018.

Internet Sites

BBC Newsround: Pangolins
bbc.co.uk/newsround/37470783

National Geographic Kids: Pangolin
kids.nationalgeographic.com/animals/mammals/facts/pangolin

One Kind Planet: Pangolin
onekindplanet.org/animal/pangolin/

Index

About the Author

Jaclyn Jaycox is a children's book author and editor. She lives in southern Minnesota with her husband, two kids, and a spunky goldendoodle.